I Hate Taking Minutes!

Published by Kogan Page Ltd, 120 Pentonville Road, London N1 9JN, UK
Website: www.kogan-page.co.uk

First published in 1997 by Fenman Ltd, reprinted with revisions by Kogan Page in 1999

Reprinted in 2002

British Library in Publication Data

A record for this book is available from the British Library.

ISBN 0 7494 2743 4

Printed by Selwood Printing Limited

Cover design by Jane Norman, Cambridge

Contents

Introduction

Very few people who have to minute meetings have had any formal training. Even those who have, find that the theory of college courses bears little resemblance to the reality of sitting in a meeting with sole responsibility for producing accurate, objective minutes.

This workbook is for anyone who takes minutes or notes. It is suitable for those who minute meetings in the workplace in both public and private sectors, and for charities, for society or club meetings. It is as appropriate for those who minute formal meetings as it is for those who are simply required to produce a list of action points from a departmental meeting.

The different styles of agenda and minutes are shown separately so that you can concentrate on the one that suits you. The book assumes no prior knowledge of minute taking in the reference sections, although some of the exercises assume that you are currently responsible for some meetings. If you are not, don't worry; just read through the exercises and come back to them in the future if you wish.

How to use the book

Above all, this is a **workbook**. This means that you are meant to write in it, to make notes, to do the exercises, and so on. Wherever possible, add your own examples, or make notes in the margin where you can 'personalise' the theory or exercises.

The book can be used in a number of ways:

1. **Quick reference**

    Use the index at the back to find the subject that concerns you and read the relevant section.

2. **Flexible learning**

    Concentrate on the subject that concerns you, working through the section and reading the reference notes.

3. **A self-study course in minute taking with model answers**

    Start at the beginning of the book and work through it. Do not try to take in too much at once. It is better to work through one section at a time and take time to understand it, rather than work though the book in one go.

4. **A reference guide**

    Read through the reference notes and highlight the points that concern you.

Note

The exercises are identified by a logo so that you can easily spot them, whether you are trying to find them or you are reading through the reference material and want to avoid them.

Use of terms

The main terms that relate to meetings are used in this **workbook** as follows:

Chairperson

The person who leads the group through the meeting.

Secretary

The person who is responsible for the administrative aspects of the meeting. This is usually setting it up, circulating the agenda, booking the room and refreshments, taking notes and circulating minutes.

Committee

Any group who meet, whether a formally constituted committee or an informal staff meeting.

Minutes

The paper or electronic record of the meeting, again irrespective of style.

1
Agenda

1.1 Setting the Agenda

Why bother with an agenda?

If you have ever been to a meeting without an agenda, you will be all too aware of the answer to this question. If there is no agenda there is no structure. Chaos rules, with participants discussing anything in any order and little is achieved.

The agenda is there to inform. It is more than just a list of items to be discussed; it can be a working document that tells members:

- what will be discussed at the meeting
- what information they should bring with them, such as papers or views of staff
- the type of decision they are expected to make.

Who is involved?

In preparing the agenda:

- participants need to be consulted regarding any items they want to discuss. This can be dealt with by circulating a note asking for items, or by having a fixed timetable that gives participants a deadline for submitting items
- consultation with the chairperson is essential to ensure that the agenda meets with his/her requirements to run the meeting properly.

Order of items in the agenda

The order of agenda items varies greatly from one organisation to another. Occasionally the order is contained in the rules of the organisation.

The format should always be logical, showing an order of priority. A typical agenda could include the following:

Heading

This must always show the name of the group, and the date, time and place of the meeting. It can also include a **reference**. This usually comprises initials to indicate the name of the group and the month or a numerical reference. Any papers which relate to the meeting should be similarly referenced so that if they get separated from the agenda or minutes it is clear what they relate to.

For example:

DPP/4.98   (Denman Place Project/April 1998 meeting or 4th meeting in 1998)
DPP/4.98-7   (Denman Place Project/April 1998 meeting or 4th meeting in 1998; paper
                relating to item 7)

The meeting can be referenced in whichever way suits the needs of the committee, but it should be as simple as possible and remain consistent.

Apologies for absence

At this stage nothing else can go here. If you do not intend numbering this section in the minutes, do not number it in the agenda.

Committee business

This section is for issues which relate to the committee as an entity rather than its objective in meeting. The changes are likely to be of the following types:

Change of personnel	(e.g. resignations, changes of office)
Change of function	(e.g. extension of remit, decision as to whether to move from advisory to active role)
Change of structure	(e.g. discussion regarding possibility of moving from only managers attending to inviting representatives from the shop floor)
Administration	(e.g. a change of quorum or frequency of meeting).

If changes are regularly made without prior notice, include Committee Business as a standing item, still in this position, as is done with Apologies.

Minutes of the previous meeting

This is for the committee to approve or make changes to the previous minutes.

Matters arising

This is for people to report back on action points from the previous minutes. Anything that needs discussion should be put as part of the main business for the meeting. It is best to make sub-headings from the previous minutes showing the initials of the person who was to take action. This will help the chairperson keep the discussion to the point.

Reports

This is for any regular reports or updates, usually on the work of members' departments or projects. Sometimes the reports originate from a matter arising but there is no longer a specific action point in the previous minutes. As a general rule, if there is an action point in the last minutes it will appear under Matters Arising in this agenda. If there is not, include it in reports. (See section 1.2 for guidance on using sub-headings to make the structure clear). Although this section can be valuable it often ends up with the members justifying their existence through lengthy presentations, if this is the case, try to avoid the section!

If the commitee is solely concerned with one project, the same agenda items may occur at every meeting. Each is likely to be an update, discussion on current problems and agreement of future action; in other words one large Matters Arising, If this is the case, omit Matters Arising as a heading and just use the appropriate headings for each item.

Main agenda items

The items for discussion at this meeting.

Any other business

This is only for items that had not arisen at the time of preparation of the agenda so nothing else can be put at this stage. Ideally a deadline for agenda items should have been included in the last minutes (under date of *Next meeting*) and anything after that date is *Any other business* on the approval of the chairman.

Next meeting

This should be simply a heading.

Chairperson's brief

A chairperson's brief is a copy of the agenda with notes giving the chairperson information needed to run the meeting effectively. This might include timings for agenda items, background information, visitors arrival times and so on.

Dispatch of agenda

An agenda needs to be dispatched in sufficient time to allow participants to prepare for the meeting.

In deciding when you send an agenda, three factors are important:

*   any rules of the organisation or committee which give a fixed timetable
*   the contribution expected from the members of the meeting, for example, to express views after consulting others
*   the frequency with which items needing the consideration of the meeting arise. Agendas comprising the same item each time need not be sent out more than a few days in advance.

Any papers that need consideration before the meeting should be circulated with the agenda. You will probably need a reminder on the agenda to encourage participants to study these before they arrive at the meeting.

Participants should be encouraged to send papers to you for dispatch with the agenda to save reading time at the meeting. The chairperson may need to reinforce this.

To avoid sending out a revised agenda, have a deadline (given under *Next meeting* in previous minutes) and use *Any other business* for items that arise after that date.

The minutes from the previous meeting should have been circulated before the agenda – it will probably be too late for participants to take action if they are only circulated at this stage (see page 44).

1.2 Styles of Agenda

There are three broad styles of agenda:

- headings
- full
- objectives.

All three are headed in the same way, showing the name of the group; the date, time and place of the meeting; the word 'agenda'.   The most common style is to display this information:

Joint Resources Committee

2 April 19XX, 9.30am-11.30am

Meeting Room 2, Bourton House

AGENDA

However, some committees prefer the older style:

A meeting of the **Joint Resources Committee** will be held on **2 April 19XX** from **9.30am** to **11.30am** in **Meeting Room 2** at **Bourton House**.

AGENDA

---

or

AGENDA for the meeting of the **Joint Resources Committee** to be held on **2 April 19XX** from **9.30am** to **11.30am** in **Meeting Room 2** at **Bourton House**.

The same style as used for the agenda should be used for the corresponding minutes:

Joint Resources Committee

2 April 19XX, 9.30am-11.30am

Meeting Room 2, Bourton House

MINUTES

> **Minutes** of the **Joint Resources Committee**, held on **2 April 19XX** from **9.30am** to **11.30am** in **Meeting Room 2** at **Bourton House**.

. . . and so on.

Headings agenda

As you would expect, a headings agenda gives the headings for the topics to be discussed:

Joint Resources Committee

2 April 19XX, 9.30am-11.30am

Meeting Room 2, Bourton House

AGENDA

1. Apologies for absence

2. Minutes of the previous meeting

3. Matters arising

4. Booking arrangements for meeting rooms

5. Installation of security cameras

6. Financial savings suggestions scheme

7. Developing the role of the secretaries

8. Any other business

9. Next meeting

Full agenda

This develops the headings agenda, giving extra information to help the participants. The example below shows who has raised the topic, or is leading the discussion (where relevant), and the papers that are attached. Perhaps the most valuable addition is the **subheadings** for the main agenda items which give a much clearer indication of what the discussion is about. Subheadings can be used to break a wide-ranging subject into simpler topics, or to group related subjects under one umbrella heading whilst retaining separate discussion.

Their use in *Matters arising* will help the chairperson keep the discussion to the report on the action points. To use subheadings here, you should refer to the action points in the last minutes and use the relevant headings with the minute number in brackets (to prevent confusion with the numbering system in this meeting). It also helps to give the initials of the person who was to take the action.

Joint Resources Committee

2 April 19XX, 9.30am-11.30am

Meeting Room 2, Bourton House

AGENDA

1. **Apologies for absence**

2. **Minutes of the previous meeting**

3. **Matters arising**

    3.1   Holiday cover for reception/switchboard (5.1)   CB

    3.2   Rotation of menus (6.2)   DD

    3.3   Office Watch scheme (8.1)   KF

    3.4   Alterations to second floor meeting rooms (9.1)   LT

4. **Booking arrangements for meeting rooms**   KA

    4.1   Problems with existing system

    4.2   Alternatives for improvement

5. **Installation of security cameras**

    Paper attached   KF

6. **Financial savings suggestions scheme**   DD

    6.1   Nature of scheme

    6.2   Administration of scheme

    6.3   Recognition of successful ideas

7. **Developing the role of the secretaries**

    7.1   Attachments with different divisions   MR

    7.2   Training for secretaries   SC

8. **Any other business**

9. **Next meeting**

Objectives agenda

An objectives agenda keeps the main headings and the other information if required. The subheadings, however, are replaced with objectives.

In theory there should be an objective for the standing items as shown in the example below. However, in practice it is enough to use them for the main agenda items. Note that the subheadings for *Matters arising* remain. The objectives can be numbered if preferred.

Joint Resources Committee

2 April 19XX, 9.30am-11.30am

Meeting Room 2, Bourton House

AGENDA

1. **Apologies for absence**

    to receive apologies for absence

2. **Minutes of the previous meeting**

    to approve minutes of meeting held on 3 March

3. **Matters arising**

    to receive reports on action points from previous minutes

3.1	Holiday cover for reception/switchboard (5.1)	CB
3.2	Rotation of menus (6.2)	DD
3.3	Office Watch scheme (8.1)	KF
3.4	Alterations to second floor meeting rooms (9.1)	LT

4. **Booking arrangements for meeting rooms**   KA

    to identify problems with existing system

    to consider alternatives for improvement

5. **Installation of security cameras**

    to decide whether to install cameras as per proposal

    Paper attached   KF

---

6. **Financial savings suggestions scheme**   DD

    to decide nature of scheme

    to agree how scheme should be administered

    to agree how successful ideas should be recognised

7. **Developing the secretarial role**

    to discuss possibility of attachments with

         different divisions   MR

    to agree training programme for secretaries   SC

8. **Any other business**

    to deal with business arising after 26 March

9. **Next meeting**

    to agree date, time and place of next meeting

Useful words for an objectives agenda

to receive	*to sit and listen*
to discuss	
to agree	
to decide	
to identify	
to consider	*no decision necessary*
to deal with	*any other business*
to approve	*previous minutes or a sub-committee decision*

 # 1.3 Preparing an Agenda

Your organisation is holding a family 'Funday' on a Sunday in a couple of months. You are secretary to the group that is planning the event. The following notes and items for the agenda have been sent to you by the group members.

Prepare both a full and an objectives agenda for the meeting so that the chairperson can select the preferred style.

Internal Memorandum

To: (name) 16.6.9X

From: Sue

Subject: FUNDAY

Is the lunch going to be a barbecue, buffet or sit-down?

Internal Memorandum

To: (name)   16.6.9X

From: Andrew

Subject: FUNDAY

Should we invite anyone from the European divisions?

Internal Memorandum

To: (name) 16.6.9X

From: Tony

Subject: FUNDAY

We must decide on children's entertainment.

Internal Memorandum

To: (name)   16.6.9X

From: Meg

Subject: FUNDAY

Venue is not available on the date.

Internal Memorandum

To: (name)   16.6.9X

From: Tony

Subject: FUNDAY

The Company magazine wants an article on the planning of the Funday.

Internal Memorandum

To: (name)   16.6.9X

From: Tony

Subject: FUNDAY

Should bar be open all day?

Internal Memorandum

To: (name) 16.6.9X

From: Meg

Subject: FUNDAY

Will bar be subsidised?

Internal Memorandum

To: (name) 16.6.9X

From: Meg

Subject: FUNDAY

Found an excellent clown, any use?

Internal Memorandum

To: (name) 16.6.9X

From: Sue

Subject: FUNDAY

Need to decide on the timetable for the day.

Internal Memorandum

To: (name) 16.6.9X

From: Sue

Subject: FUNDAY

The French division want an article for their magazine as they are planning a similar event in the spring next year.

Internal Memorandum

To: (name) 16.6.9X

From: Alison

Subject: FUNDAY

Select the caterers, get away from staff canteen style this year.

Internal Memorandum

To: (name) 16.6.9X

From: Alison

Subject: FUNDAY

Got offer of a huge barbecue; do we want it?

Before your next meeting . . .

1 Decide which style of agenda you would prefer and identify the reasons why.

2 Prepare the agenda in this style or in a couple of styles to show the chairperson.

3 Introduce changes slowly if you wish, for example, introduce subheadings where necessary and build up the style.

2
The Meeting

2.1 Preparation for a Meeting

Some time spent in preparation for a meeting will help you take accurate notes which will save you precious time in writing up the minutes.

Before you turn the page, list as many ways as you can think of to prepare for a meeting.

I can invest time in preparing for a meeting by:

For example: Reading minutes of previous meeting.

1. _____

2. _____

3. _____

4. _____

5. _____

6. _____

7. _____

8. _____

9. _____

10. _____

The tasks below will take a bit of time, but if you do them you will reduce stress, improve your minutes and save time in the long run.

Read through the minutes of the previous meeting

Even if you wrote the minutes, reading through them will remind you of the discussion and the people involved and will familiarise you with the subject and any technical terms.

Confirm the admin. arrangements

You will not only look professional if you are up to date with the coffee arrangements, the expected finish time, the workings of the overhead projector and so on, but you will also have peace of mind!

Read through the agenda

Again, reading the agenda will familiarise you with the content.

Read any papers that relate to the meeting

Familiarity aids understanding. By reading through and studying any technical terms you will find it easier to listen and to understand. You will also be able to relax from note-taking and simply mark on your copy of the paper what is being said.

Who's who?

If you do not know everyone who is attending, read through the names and picture those you do know. If necessary, mark those you don't know so that you are ready to 'pick them off' and put a name to a face as it becomes clear who is who.

If possible, ask around to find out about those you don't know to help with identification at the meeting.

Check supplies

You should take a pen (or pens) that you like writing with and paper that you like writing on. Take a clipboard if you will not be sitting at a table. It is worth taking extra supplies as you will often be regarded as a stationery cupboard by forgetful participants.

Take master copies

If you regularly have to make extra copies, take a clean white master copy of each piece of paper, printed on one side only – it will make copying much quicker. You will also probably need extra copies of the agenda and minutes for those who 'didn't receive theirs'.

Take the minutes for signing

If the minutes are to be signed, take the appropriate copy with you. Remember that it should be initialled on each page if it is not bound.

Note things to discuss with the chairperson

For example, you may wish to ask what type of minutes are required (*see section 4.1*). Are you able to interrupt if you miss something? More importantly, you can ask the chairperson for the help you need. For example, you could ask for each participant to give their name before speaking, or for the chairperson to summarise each discussion for the minutes, or for the coffee to be poured before the start of the meeting. It may be counter-productive to have too long a list but you can gently train the chairperson to lead the meeting in a way which helps you (and the other participants).

Consider what to wear

You need to 'fit in' if you are to be accepted and to have your minutes respected by the group. You should also take care to avoid bracelets or loose watches, cuff buttons and so on which rattle and can be a distraction to you and to others.

Before your next meeting . . .

Prepare a checklist of:

- what to do in advance

- what to find out from the chairperson

- what the chairperson could do to help you and how you are going to ask for this help.

2.2 At the Meeting

The list below contains some of the most common problems that a minute taker faces at a meeting. Consider each one and decide what can be done to minimise or overcome it. In the spaces at the end, add any additional problems you face and give some constructive thought to these as well.

Common problem	Ideas to help
Finding out who's who	_____
	_____
	_____
	_____
Remembering who's who	_____
	_____
	_____
	_____
Staying awake	_____
	_____
	_____
	_____
Hearing what is said	_____
	_____
	_____
	_____
Not understanding	_____
	_____
	_____
	_____

Common problem	Ideas to help
Everybody arguing	_____
	_____
	_____
	_____
Can I interrupt?	_____
	_____
	_____
Being sent out to copy	_____
	_____
	_____
	_____
Coffee	_____
	_____
	_____
Where to sit	_____
	_____
	_____
	_____
Being a working member of the group as well as a note taker	_____
	_____
	_____
	_____
	_____

Common problem	Ideas to help
Other 1	_____
	_____
	_____
	_____
2	_____
	_____
	_____
	_____

Ideas to help

Finding out who's who

- Do not be afraid to ask, either the chairperson or someone else you know.

- Introduce yourself; you will find out who people are and you will give the impression of social confidence.

- When everyone is seated, pass around a sheet of paper and ask that everyone **prints** their name and job title, *but*:

   1. print the chairperson's or your name first, otherwise if the first person merely signs their name, the others will follow

   2. watch for and mark on the list any empty seats. Most people do not leave a space as the paper goes round and if a seat is subsequently filled your list will be out of order.

Remembering who's who

- Familiarise yourself with the names before you attend the meeting.

- Make a seating plan and mark in the people you know. Add in other names as you remember them or when others call them by name.

- Use name-plates, either pre-prepared or fold A5 sheets of card and provide thick pens.

- Having been introduced to someone, use their name once whilst you are talking to them.

   For example: 'Do you work at the Albion Road site <u>Mr Jones</u>?"

- Look at people as they are talking and consciously think of their names.

- In an address book keep a note of the people who attend meetings.

Include where they work, their job and something about their appearance (be positive!). When vaguely familiar names crop up in the future you can check back.

Staying awake

- Sit straight.

- Maintain eye contact with each person who speaks. Apart from keeping you awake, this encourages the speaker to include you in their 'audience', which makes hearing easier and you appear more confident.

- Avoid doodling. Doodling often leads to day dreaming, which in turn leads to heavy lids.

- During a break, escape to the toilet and run cold water on your inner wrists.

- Make sure you are not too warm and that there is fresh air (if possible) in the room.

Hearing what is said

- Eye contact – everybody lip-reads to some extent.

- Focus on the speaker and cut out other noise.

- Sit beside the chairperson; most speech will be directed that way.

Not understanding

Remember that you are unlikely to have the in-depth subject knowledge that participants may have, so there is no shame in not understanding technical points.

- Familiarise yourself with the previous minutes before the meeting.

- Write down in your own words what the group is talking about (or at least who was speaking) so that you have some clue when you have to ask a question.

- Devise a system for indicating words that you are unsure of in your notes to remind yourself to look them up or to check them with someone.

- Warn the chairperson in advance that you do not have specific technical knowledge and ask them to explain terms beforehand or afterwards.

- Ask the individual concerned to brief you before the meeting or to explain important points after it.

Everybody arguing

- Note down what the argument is about.

- Concentrate on the opinion of one person at a time, and note, that until the minutes reflect the views of each contributor (see page 21).

Can I interrupt?

- Ask the chairperson.

- Only interrupt when you have not heard something, when you need to clarify a point or when you need a summary for the minutes (probably because you have not understood a rambling point!).

Being sent out to copy

- Try to agree with the chairperson in advance that someone else should do this and similar tasks.

- Pass the minutes to the person sitting next to you, ideally the chairperson, and ask clearly, warmly and politely (with good eye contact) that they take the notes until you return.

Coffee

- Leave coffee on a trolley or side table for people to help themselves before the meeting starts.

- If you are directly asked to serve the coffee, pass the minutes on as above while you are serving. Then sort this one out with the chairperson before next time.

- If you suffer from shaky hands, and thus rattling cups, make sure that you move firmly and decisively. If nothing else, this will leave less time to rattle!

- If the coffee is shunted towards you on the assumption that you will pour, thank the 'shunter', pour your own and shunt it onwards.

Where to sit

- Next to the chairperson! You are the two people sharing responsibility for the running of the meeting.

Being a working member of the committee as well as a note taker

- Note when you spoke, rather than the point you were making; you should be able to remember the latter in context.

- Concentrate on being objective and fair in your summary.

- Do not be afraid to 'pause' the meeting while you make a note at the end of the discussion.

- Try to circulate the note taking role amongst the group.

- If you are the **chairperson**, clearly summarise the discussion at the end of each item and then note the summary. If you do this into a dictaphone people are more likely to be quiet and wait rather than move on to the next item or re-start the closed discussion.

Before your next meeting . . .

1. Identify the problems that you most commonly have and plan your strategy for removing or reducing them.

2. Identify the information you need from the chairperson.

3. Identify the things the chairperson could do to make your role easier.

4. Plan how you can ask for the above in the most positive way and then arrange a brief meeting or informal encounter.

5. Remember that if you look confident, the committee will have greater confidence in your minutes. They will also treat you more professionally which, in turn, adds to your confidence.

3

Writing it Down

3.1 Listening and Summarising

It is essential to get away from 'taking dictation' when note taking. If you struggle to keep up and end up with pages of scribble this is likely to be your problem.

It is not the words a person is using that matter, it is what they are talking about (the subject) and their viewpoint that is important.

Much of what is said in meetings consists of:

- expressing a viewpoint

- illustrating or supporting that view

- re-stating the view, perhaps in stronger terms and/or with different examples.

It is the **viewpoint** that you should be listening for and noting.

For example:

Quote from Tom	Noted as
"In my department it won't work. To list every item in the post is a waste of my staff's time and everyone has enough to do already."	Tom: disagrees, waste of staff time*
Later in the discussion "I don't think it's necessary – I cannot remember the last time we lost any post."	Tom: don't lose post now*
Later again "It is going to delay things too much. We don't get our post now until coffee time. If it all has to be booked in, we'll be lucky to see it before lunch."	Tom: will delay post more*
• *This example shows how you would take notes if you were expected to minute the reasons. However, you may not necessarily want to do this. In this case, just note something like, "There were a number of reasons given for opposing the idea that . . ."*	

Make sure that the subject (which in the example above is the booking in of post) is highlighted by circling or underlining it. Similarly, highlight the viewpoints so that they stand out (in Tom's case, the word 'disagrees'). This will make your notes considerably easier to re-read later.

Try to note a person's viewpoint once only. If you leave a fair amount of space you can return to add extra notes if you wish (see page 25).

One important aspect of recognising the subject and viewpoint is the ability to recognise the irrelevant.

A person's words are likely to be irrelevant on two grounds:

1.   they have already made the point and you have noted it

2.   their words bear no relevance to the discussion.

3.2 Subject and Viewpoint

Identify the subject (and, where given, the viewpoint) in the following statements. They are not related.

1. "I think we should introduce a 'post-in' system so that we can easily track all mail."

2. "Tom came to see me yesterday and asked what we are going to do about the Christmas shut down."

3. "None of my staff likes the idea of an open-plan office and I am having a hard time convincing them of the benefits. I think we should reconsider."

4. "Jackie is a fine manager and her tactful approach has worked wonders on morale in that department."

5. "If we allow the flexitime to be extended to administrative staff, there will be no stopping it. Soon the production lines will be stopping and starting at random."

3.3 Summarising a Report

Write a summary minute for the following extract of a paper that was attached to an agenda and presented at a meeting.

Annual Report: Health and Safety

Ted Jordan, Health and Safety Manager gave his annual report. The training programme finished in March and over 70% of staff attended. The remainder either missed the sessions due to sickness or could not be released to attend. The high percentage of staff who did not attend is disappointing.

During the year there have been four accidents which resulted in staff needing to take time off work. In February, Mrs M Barker slipped down the three steps leading from the canteen and broke her left arm. In March, Miss D Slocombe mixed cleaning fluids during a major clean up of the third floor toilets and suffered breathing difficulties. In August, Mr V Adams broke his toe in an accident on the shop floor; he had dropped a can of paint. In October, Mrs D Lyons broke her arm whilst running up the main staircase. In none of these cases was there any suggestion that the company was responsible.

A new Health and Safety Training Programme is to be implemented, again with one-day general courses for staff who have received no previous training and half-day refresher courses for those who attended the sessions last year.   There will also be specific courses for those who want or need to develop their knowledge (for example, Lifting Skills, Conveyor-belt Safety). These will be arranged as required.

Develop your skills

Listen to the radio or TV news and identify what each story is about. (This is good practice for spotting the subject.)

As you listen to conversations around you, identify what the person is talking about and what their viewpoint is. This can also be done with radio or TV interviews, chat shows and so on.

3.4 Taking Notes

Once you can identify the difference between a subject, a viewpoint and examples, you can give some thought as to how you arrange your notes. There is no right or wrong way. It is simply a matter of personal preference. This section outlines four alternative methods, based around this extract from a meeting to consider the problems of car-parking:

Douglas:	"Too many staff are parking on the road."
Tony:	"I watched a lorry having trouble reversing in, that often happens."
Merula:	"It's hardly surprising as the car park gets full by 8.15."
Douglas:	"Lower spaces are available, it's just that the road is nearer and people are too lazy to walk uphill."
Tony:	"Does it matter? After all, it's not a main road and there aren't any yellow lines."
Douglas:	"Of course it matters, it is really difficult to see coming in and out; there will be an accident one day and we'll probably get the blame."
Tony:	"Well, there are usually spaces in the directors' bays."
Merula:	"And the visitors' car park has ten bays but usually only a couple of cars."
Tony:	"Why not double up the directors' and visitors' car parks?"
Merula:	"We would have to do away with named bays for the directors."
Douglas:	"We do need to get people to use the lower spaces; how can we do this?"

Simple scribble

This method involves writing on A4 paper or a notepad, using the whole page.

STAFF PARKING

D – too many staff parking on road

T – lorries have problems

M – car park full by 8.15

D – lower spaces available staff too lazy

T – not a main road no yellow lines

D – dangerous will be an accident

T – spaces in directors' bays

M – and in visitors' car park

T – double up directors' and visitors' car parks?

M – couldn't have marked bays

D – get people to use lower spaces – how?

Structured scribble

Divide each A4 page into four vertical columns:

- The first, often the margin, is used to note the agenda item number under discussion.

- The second is the largest, preferably about half the page width, and is for writing the notes.

- The third is for going back to notes to add additional examples, like supporting comments from colleagues.

- The fourth is for noting outcomes and actions when agreed.

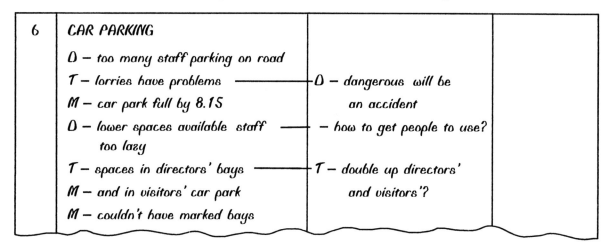

Seating plan

This can only work with a small meeting, say three or four people. For each discussion draw a table plan and note subjects and viewpoints alongside names.

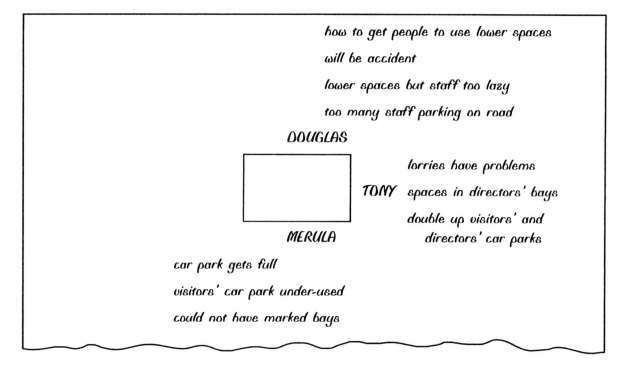

As you can see, it is difficult to follow the logic of a forward-moving discussion like this when using a seating plan. However, it is useful when the discussion involves everyone giving their opinions. (For example, on how to cut overtime!)

You will often need to combine this style with the subject structure below as during meetings ideas can be contradicted. This would develop the seating plan to something like the example below:

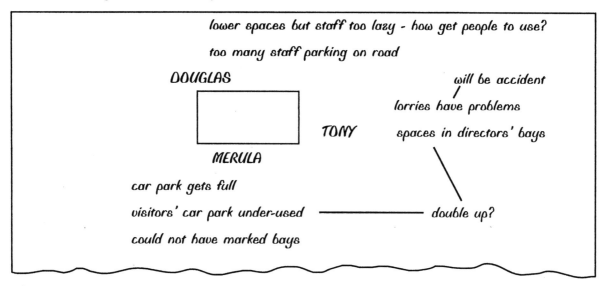

As you can see, this will quickly become muddled. Keep it for occasions when participants are asked to simply give ideas or opinions with little or no discussion.

A variation of this is **for and against.** Participants split into two or three 'camps', for example, those for and against an idea, or in favour of a seven-day or ten-day period. You can divide your notes as you take them:

Extend flexitime to admin and secretarial staff?

FOR	AGAINST
Note who is in favour and any relevant comments.	Note who is against and any relevant comments.
or	or
Who is in favour of a seven-day period.	Who is in favour of a ten-day period.
Neutral comments and general points can be written across the middle.	

Subject structure

Whereas the seating plan approach is based on grouping the views of people, displayed as where they are sitting, the subject structure displays the discussion according to the content of their views (commonly known as a mind map or spidergram). This is a more logical and practical way of noting a discussion.

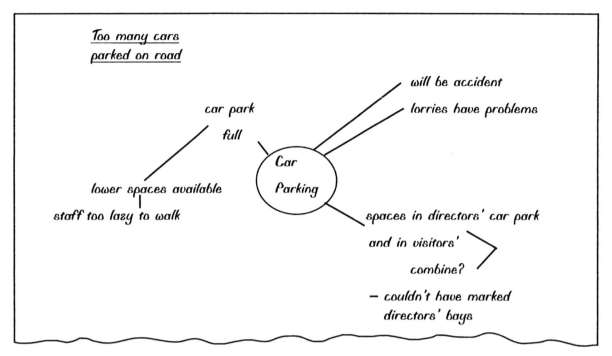

In summary, there is no 'right' method. Different methods will suit different types of discussion. Where someone is presenting a report, **simple scribble** may be adequate. (However, this is the least useful method in general because for discussion, it is muddled and difficult to read back.)

In general discussion, **structured scribble** is the most helpful because you can return to a viewpoint and add to it or simply put the initials of a participant who is agreeing with that view.

A **seating plan** works well where ideas are being generated or where each participant is required to give their views on an issue.

In a discussion where the views fall into two or three fairly well defined camps, use the **for and against** version.

If you are used to drawing mind maps or have a creative way of thinking, a **subject structure** will suit you.

When taking notes, you will probably find that you can use two or three styles (if not more) in a single meeting, based on the type of discussion - this is the right way!

Writing up your notes

The earlier you can write up your notes, the easier it will be. If, however, pressure of work makes this difficult, consider the following options:

- If the meeting had gone on for another 15 minutes, you would have been correspondingly later back to your desk. Try to find a few extra minutes *before* you return to your office to read through and add to your notes.

- Type notes quickly onto the word processor, ignoring mistakes, gaps and so on. Add in other points, identify places where you know there is a problem, and so on. You may find it easier to work from this when you come to write up the minutes.

- Dictate your notes into a dictaphone, again, as they appear and work from this to write up the minutes.

Before your next meeting . . .

1 Spend a few minutes listening to conversations around you in the office. Takes notes of one or two of them.

2 Tape news or discussion programmes from the radio and TV and take notes, using the tape to check your accuracy. This is legal for private study.

3 Take these notes in as many of the styles as you can. Practice means that you can swap quickly in a meeting.

4 If you find it hard to get away from simple scribble, rule up the page and move to structured scribble. You will usually find that it is possible to include one of the other styles in a simple way when the discussion is appropriate.

3.5 Taking Notes

Read through the script below and then minute the discussion in the *simple scribble, for and against,* and *subject structure* methods together with any other style you want to try. Which works the best?

Chair:	Annie, you wanted to discuss water machines.
Annie:	Yes, thank you. I was visiting a supplier last week; excellent meeting – that new guy, Alistair Greening, is really clued up! Anyway after the usual coffee, he pointed out a drinking water machine and said to help myself if I wanted any.
Nathan:	I've seen them, they're good.
Simon:	Particularly for us non-coffee drinkers.
Annie:	Anyway, I thought they would be a good idea for the meeting rooms.
Simon:	Excellent idea, let's go ahead.
Liz:	What's the cost?
Nathan:	Oh, I don't think it's too much – probably less than we spend on the bottled water we have now.
Annie:	And at least it will be chilled.
Liz:	Have you any idea of the cost?
Annie:	Catalogue price is a unit rental of £3 per week plus £7 for a bottle of water.
Liz:	That's not too bad.
Nathan:	Won't we use a lot more water because it will be on hand rather than having to be ordered specifically from catering.
Liz:	We have many bottles returned with only a glass or two taken out and the rest is wasted. People don't drink water for the sake of it.
Simon:	We will have to raise the rate for room hire.
Liz:	We can cover it for the rest of the year and raise the charge by a little more at the usual time. I don't see it as a problem – they happily pay for bottled water.
Andy:	Who is going to be responsible for replacing the bottles? They're going to be heavy.
Annie:	The caretakers could do it when they lock up and could be called upon for mid-day replacements if necessary.
Liz:	I'm sure they would be happy to do that and catering would be responsible for buying.

Chair:	Are we in favour of installing these machines in the seven meeting rooms with catering to negotiate price to a current maximum of £3 and £7 as we said, and with the caretakers to take responsibility for maintenance?

General agreement

Chair:	Liz, this seems to be an action point for you.
Liz:	I'll phone the suppliers and report back to the next meeting. I will have them installed before then if possible.
Simon:	You'd better forewarn the caretakers, too!
Liz:	I'll do that.

4

The Minutes

4.1 Styles of Minutes

There are three broad styles of minutes:

*   verbatim

*   summary

*   action.

All provide a record of the meeting, show the outcome of the discussion and who will take action. The difference is in the presentation of the discussion.

Verbatim minutes

It would not be possible to produce minutes that were truly 'word for word' without shorthand at around 180wpm, astounding concentration and a committee who spoke one at a time.

In fact, verbatim minutes are the 'she said, he said' type, where individuals' views are summarised. Their advantage is that they show the background to decisions in detail, but this is often outweighed by the fact that they are long, very involved and leave the minute taker open to the charge of 'I didn't say that'. Although names are often given, they need not be. They can be replaced with phrases such as 'it was stated that' or 'the committee heard that'.

Minutes where each angle of the discussion is outlined are also classed as verbatim. For example, where every problem is detailed rather than the more general summary along the lines of 'The committee discussed possible problems but . . .'

Example verbatim minute (with names)

Attachments to different divisions

Mike Readwin suggested that the secretaries should have the opportunity of short attachments to other divisions. This would operate in the same way as the managers' 'Attachments' programme. Lesley Thompson asked what the point of this was since the managers used the scheme to gain experience prior to promotion. Mike explained that the secretaries would find out how other divisions worked and gain a greater understanding of how the organisation worked. Communication across the divisions would benefit and best practice could be shared.

Khalid Ahmal asked how the system would work and Mike suggested that the attachments would be limited to a two- or three-week period. Khalid asked who would cover for the secretaries and suggested that rather than an attachment, there should be a job swap. This was supported by Sue Cotterell who pointed out that otherwise there would be times when in one department two secretaries were doing the work of one whilst no one was doing the work in the other department.

Lesley pointed out the problems of confidentiality and of a grade three secretary taking on the role of a grade four secretary, perhaps without the skills to cope. Toby Maxwell suggested that the issue of confidentiality was no different than that for the managers and that with regard to the grading, it often bore little relation to the work undertaken and in any event the 'real' secretary would be within the building.

Toby suggested that a consultation e-mail be circulated to the secretaries asking for their views and suggestions on how a scheme might work. If the outcome from this was positive, the proposal would be put to the director.

ACTION: MIKE READWIN

Example verbatim minute (without names)

Attachments to different divisions

The committee considered the possibility of the secretaries having the opportunity of short attachments to other divisions. This would operate in the same way as the managers' 'Attachments' programme. It was suggested that there was little point as the managers used the scheme to gain experience prior to promotion. It was explained that the secretaries would find out how other divisions worked and gain a greater understanding of how the organisation worked. Communication across the divisions would benefit and best practice could be shared.

The workings of the system were considered and the suggestion was that the attachments would be limited to a two- or three-week period. Because of the problems of cover for the secretaries it was suggested that rather than an attachment, there should be a job swap. There was support for this because otherwise there would be times when in one department two secretaries were doing the work of one whilst no one was doing the work in the other department.

Confidentiality and the possibility of a grade three secretary taking on the role of a grade four secretary, perhaps without the skills to cope were discussed. However, the issue of confidentiality was felt to be no different than that for the managers and that with regard to the grading, it often bore little relation to the work undertaken and in any event the 'real' secretary would be within the building.

It was decided that a consultation e-mail be circulated to the secretaries asking for their views and suggestions on how a scheme might work. If the outcome from this was positive, the proposal would be put to the director.

ACTION: MIKE READWIN

Summary minutes

Summary minutes are by far the most popular. This is because they are shorter, easier to take and quicker to read. They summarise the discussion as a whole without getting into too much detail so, for example, 'he said, she said' is replaced with, 'the committee discussed'.

The minutes are focused more on the subject (what the committee is talking about) than on the individuals (what people are saying).

They are much easier to note because there is no requirement to write everything down. Also, they have the benefit of avoiding the minute-taker being faced with 'I didn't say that'. They also give a better summary because the domination of an over-enthusiastic participant is not obvious.

Example summary minute

Attachments to different divisions

The committee discussed the possibility of the 'Attachments' programme being broadened to include secretaries. This would benefit the secretaries through experience of how others worked and a greater overall understanding of the organisation. This would benefit their managers and communication across the divisions would be improved.

A job swap was felt to be better than an attachment to ensure even cover. The problems of confidentiality and mixing grades were considered but felt to be not serious.

The committee decided to circulate a consultation e-mail to secretaries, asking for their views and suggestions on how a scheme might work. If the outcome from this was positive, the proposal would be put to the director.

ACTION: MIKE READWIN

Action minutes

Action minutes simply show the heading, the decision and who is to take the action. They are very simple to take and, being very short and action-centred, are easy to read. They are not so valuable if many members of the committee did not attend the meeting. In addition, they provide no view of how a decision was reached, but are excellent where only a reminder is required.

Example action minutes

Attachments to different divisions

It was decided to circulate a consultation e-mail to secretaries, asking for their views and suggestions on how a scheme might work. If the outcome from this was positive, the proposal would be put to the director

     ACTION: MIKE READWIN

4.2 Using the Styles

1.   Write the minutes for the following discussion in each of the three styles
     a) verbatim, b) action and c) summary.

John:	Suggested allowing secretarial staff to take up to one hour unofficial flexitime by finishing at 3.00pm on Friday.
Sue:	Won't work as no one will be around to cover on Fridays.
Ali:	Secretaries could arrange cover – no cover = not leave early.
Martin:	Thin end of wedge ... next thing will be all Friday afternoon off.
Sue:	Or full-scale flexitime.
John:	A bad thing?
Ali:	Never considered ... too big a decision for this meeting and now.
Malcolm:	Not a major perk. Some departments have informal arrangements now. J's suggestion seems a small and limited move.
Sue:	Can it be limited to one hour on Friday? Not happy about staff disappearing anytime.
John:	No reason why not.
Martin:	If limited to one hour on Friday – go along with it.
Sue:	Suppose so.
John:	Agreed? Staff on grades 1-4 can take up to one hour in lieu of overtime on a Friday afternoon secretaries to arrange cover?
General 'yes'.	

2.   Return to the discussion on water machines in the exercise on page 30
     and, using your preferred styles of notes, again write the minutes of the
     discussion in each of the three styles.

4.3 Sections of Minutes

The different sections of the minutes are taken from the agenda and should be headed and numbered in the same way. Although the firm rules for each section have relaxed in many cases, there are still some conventions to be followed.

Apologies

Although of the five sections listed below, only *Apologies* appears in the agenda, they are all related. Every name should appear under one of the headings, so that together they provide a complete record and circulation list. Examples of different layouts are shown below.

Present

This lists members of the committee who attended the meeting. If they attended only part of the meeting, this should be shown.

For example: Francesca Laurence   (to item 6)

This shows observers – those who watch the meeting but are not allowed to participate.

In attendance

This lists anyone else who attended the meeting. The minute taker is 'in attendance' unless they are a member of the group and take the minutes in addition to their role within the meeting (in which case they are present). Again, if anyone attended only part of the meeting, this should be shown.

For example: Dr Peter Ranshaw   (item 3)

Apologies

This lists members of the committee who let the chairperson or secretary know, in advance, that they would not attend, or who sent their apologies with another committee member.

Absent

This lists members who did not send apologies and did not attend the meeting. Although use of 'Absent' can cause offence (and protestations that they did tell someone), it is an effective way of spotlighting people who regularly fail to attend without advising you.

Copy to

This lists anyone who receives the minutes but does not attend the meetings.

By using these six sections, you have a full mailing list for minutes and future agenda. You also provide a historical record of everyone who was involved in the committee. You do not have to show all sections, the ones you do not need can simply be omitted.

Numbering of Apologies

If you intend to display *Apologies*, along with *Present* and any of the other sections above (rather than have it as the first item in the minutes), remember not to number it in the agenda.

Examples:

The following examples demonstrate the use of and show the different layouts for *apologies*. Any of these formats is acceptable, but, whichever you choose, be consistent.

A second (or even third) column for the names will sometimes be necessary to prevent this section from taking up most of the page.

MINUTES

Present: Alice Berenson   (chair)

                 Marcus Dixon

                 Adrian Lewis

                 Simon Palmer

                 Toby Shell   Copy to: Adrian Lewis

In attendance: Tom Harris
                 Sheila Lane (minutes)

1.   **Apologies for absence**

       Apologies were received from Vicky Marshall and Chris Green was absent.

Apologies must have been numbered in the agenda and this has carried over to the minutes.

MINUTES

Present:	Alice Berenson	(Chair)
	Marcus Dixon	
	Adrian Lewis	
	Simon Palmer	
	Toby Shell	
In attendance:	Tom Harris	
	Sheila Lane (Minutes)	
Apologies:	Vicky Marshall	
Absent:	Chris Green	
Copy to:	Adrian Lewis	

1. Minutes of Previous Meeting

Apologies must not be numbered in the agenda if the minutes are to be laid out in this format.

MINUTES

Present:	Alice Berenson	(Chair)	
	Marcus Dixon	Apologies:	Vicky Marshall
	Adrian Lewis	Absent:	Chris Green
	Simon Palmer		
	Toby Shell	Copy to:	Adrian Lewis
In attendance:	Tom Harris		
	Sheila Lane (Minutes)		

1.   Minutes of Previous Meeting

Apologies must not be numbered in the agenda if the minutes are to be laid out in this format.

Committee business

Any changes to the structure, personnel or constitution of the committee should be minuted within this section. The most common areas are probably resignations and discussions regarding staff replacements. By keeping such discussions to this section, they are separated out from the working business of the committee.

Minutes of the previous meeting

When the minutes are approved, the wording should be along the lines of:

> "The minutes of the meeting held on (date) were approved as a true and accurate record."

If there are changes, these should be minuted under the appropriate subheading with the correct version highlighted.

For example: **Arrangements for Christmas shut down**

Item 6.1 to be amended to read "The office will re-open on Monday 5th January . . . "

The final paragraph then becomes:

> "... were subsequently approved as a true and accurate record."

Matters arising

This section should contain brief notes to confirm that action from previous minutes has been taken, is in hand or detail when/how it will be taken. Subheadings should be taken from the previous minutes (see below and page 42 for examples). Anything requiring discussion should be included in the main business of the committee.

If discussion re-starts on an item which was decided upon at the previous meeting (and therefore minuted), it should not be minuted again at the current meeting unless the outcome is different.

Matters arising can either be minuted under subheadings as above, or can be displayed in a table.

For example:

Minuted under subheadings

3.   Matters Arising
3.1   **Problems with existing system** (4.1)
To canvass users and compile a list of specific problems. - K.A.
Completed, discussed as Item 6 below.
3.2   **Installation of security cameras** (5)
To instruct Aceview Security to proceed as per quotation. - K.F.
Cameras to be installed by end of May.

3.3 **Training for Secretaries** (7.2)

Investigate alternatives for in-house training. - S.C.

Literature being collated. Series of meetings being set up with possible providers.

Minuted as a table

3 Matters Arising

Item	Heading	Action	By	Status
4.1	Problems with existing system.	To canvass users and compile a list of specific problems	K.A.	Completed, discussed as Item 6 below.
5	Installation of security cameras.	To instruct Aceview Security to proceed as per quotation.	K.F.	Cameras to be installed by end of May.
7.2	Training for secretaries	Investigate alternatives for in-house training.	S.C.	Literature being collated. Series of meetings being set up with possible providers.

Reports or standing items

If various members of staff give regular reports, this is where they should be minuted. If the reports are written and circulated, there is no need to minute the content.

Some committees have items that are discussed at each meeting. It is generally best to deal with these first to separate them from the new or current issues.

Main agenda items

Minutes may either reflect the order in which the business was dealt with at the meeting or, more commonly, the order as it appeared on the agenda. If the order is changed you can either:

1. type the minutes in numerical order from the agenda and preface them with "The following items were discussed in the order: 1, 2, 6, 4, 7, 5";

or

2. type the minutes in the order in which they were discussed (keeping the original agenda numbers for each topic) and preface them with "The items were discussed in the following order: item 1, item 2, item 6" and so on.

Whatever the order adopted, each item in a minute should be clearly numbered and titled. The headings will be taken from the agenda, but it is advisable to add in subheadings to facilitate the location of information.

Tense

Minutes must always be presented in the past tense; you are reporting on a meeting that has taken place.

Use of names

Today it is acceptable to use names of contributors in minutes, but it is preferable to avoid your minutes becoming a list of 'he said' and 'she said' with a summary of each contributor's views.

Initials are best avoided unless **everyone** who will read the minutes is familiar with **all** initials. Whether you choose to use Mr or Mrs, a title, first names or full names, be consistent.

Generally it is best to keep to Mr/Mrs in more formal minutes and use first and surnames for informal ones. With the latter, use the full name once but if it appears again in the same minute item, you can use first name only.

Numbers

Numbers up to 10 must be written out in full and you may wish to do the same for numbers between 10 and 20. Numbers up to 10 can be written as numbers if they are expressed as money or a percentage but any number that starts a sentence should be written in full.

Minuting insults and heated discussion

Personal insults should not be minuted, even in verbatim minutes. However, listen to see if there is a genuine point being expressed in a rather too forthright manner.

For example:

"Your department is like a bloody bull in a china shop."

is best ignored; whereas:

"Your department is like a bloody bull in a china shop, you barge in without finding out the facts first."

could be minuted as:

"The importance of finding out the facts before acting was stressed and ..."

Being asked to minute a specific point

If a member of the committee asks that their specific point is minuted, you should refer to the chairperson for approval.

Any other business

Items should be given appropriate subheadings and be minuted as above.

Next meeting

The date, time and venue for the next meeting should be noted. It is also helpful to give a deadline for agenda items.

After the meeting

Tidy up and write up your notes as soon as possible (see page 28). The minutes should be checked by the chairperson before they are circulated to the committee. Avoid having them checked by the individual participants, as you are always certain to end up with conflicting amendments.

Dispatch of minutes

Since one of the main purposes of minutes is to remind participants of actions they must take, it is important to dispatch the minutes as soon as possible, ideally so that they arrive earlier than half-way towards the next meeting.

If it is not possible to do this, copy across the action points (to form basic action minutes) and dispatch this swiftly.

4.4 Recording Decisions and Actions

It is important to be clear about the difference between 'decision' and 'action'.

Decision

This is the outcome of a discussion – what the committee have agreed to do or not do. The decision can be incorporated into the summary (although it should be a separate paragraph) or can be given a separate heading to ensure that it does not get lost in the text.

For example:

> The committee agreed to send a copy to the Management Team and ask whether there was any reason not to circulate to all departments before the break.

or

> **Agreed:**   To send a copy to the Management Team and ask whether there was any reason not to circulate to all departments before the break.

Useful words

Many words can be used to show the outcome of discussion. Some are:

The Committee ...	agreed	*where some other body has to approve the action*
	resolved	*where the committee has the authority to take the action*
	decided to	*can be used in either of the above circumstance*
	approved	*... the recommendation that ...*
	deferred	*... the matter to a later meeting*
	referred	*... the matter to another body*
	implemented	*put to effect*
	established	*secured, or settled that*
	set up	*started something*

('Agreed', 'resolved' and 'decided' are generally interchangeable these days.)

Action

This shows who is to carry out the decision. Again, it can be displayed in a number of ways but to ensure success, the name and deadline for the action should be given.

A popular way of highlighting actions is to use an 'Action' column in the right-hand margin of the page. This has the advantage of showing the name or initials of the person clearly, but the disadvantage is that it wastes a considerable amount of paper and may need to be prepared as a table. This causes difficulties where different size fonts are used, or if there are amendments

There are two alternatives to making the 'Action' column. The first is to show the actions underneath the text and indent them. The second is to have an action column on the left-hand margin, using hanging indents.

For example:

Action column in the right-hand margin

The committee agreed to send a copy to the Management Team and ask whether there was any reason not to circulate to all departments before the break.	**Kerry Waldron** **29/11/98**

Action shown underneath the text and indented

The committee agreed to send a copy to the Management Team and ask whether there was any reason not to circulate to all departments before the break.

Action: Kerry Waldron by 29/11/98

Variation on the above

The committee agreed to send a copy to the Management Team and ask whether there was any reason not to circulate to all departments before the break.

Action: Kerry Waldron

Deadline: 29/11/98

Action column on the left-hand margin, with an alternative way of showing name and deadline.

> **KW** (29/11/98)   The committee agreed to send a copy to the Management Team and ask whether there was any reason not to circulate to all departments before the break.

Combining decision and action

If you need to have quite a lot of detail of the discussion, it is best to separate decision and action from the rest of the details. This can be done as below:

Decision and action separated out and indented

> ... reminded the committee that there was no formal requirement to have the document approved by the Management Team but agreed that its support would be valuable.
>
> **Agreed:**   To send a copy to the Management Team and ask whether there was any reason not to circulate to all departments before the break.
>
> **Action:**   **Kerry Waldron** by 29/11/98

> ... reminded the committee that there was no formal requirement to have the document approved by the Management Team but agreed that its support would be valuable.

Decision	Deadline	Action by
To send a copy to the Management Team and ask whether there was any reason not to circulate to all departments before the break.	*29 November 98*	*Kerry Waldron*

Note that 'decision' can be replaced by 'agreed' or 'resolved'.

Where there is no decision

Where the discussion draws to a close with no decision being reached (as opposed to a specific decision to defer or to do nothing) this should be recorded. The usual wording for this is 'no decision was reached'.

This differs from 'no action to be taken' (which represents a decision to do nothing) or 'no further action required'.

4.5 Headings and Numbering

Committee members may be too busy (and perhaps not sufficiently interested) to read your minutes in depth. They may scan through them, looking for their name and any areas of particular interest. Headings will help them to do so quickly and easily.

The numbering also helps, both by showing which are main and which are subheadings and for quick reference for those who know the number of agenda items at the meeting.

Headings

The headings and subheadings used in the agenda must always be used in the minutes. It is therefore worth giving careful thought to these when you prepare the agenda.

In addition to these agenda originated headings, it is very helpful to add subheadings in the minutes.

As a very broad rule of thumb, try not to have more than three paragraphs without using a subheading. To choose your headings, read through the paragraph and ask yourself "what is this about?"

Numbering

The three most usual styles of numbering are:

To start each agenda with number one and continue in sequence. This has the advantage of simplicity.

For example: 7. **Maintenance Contract**

To start the first agenda of the year with number one and number continuously from there. The number is usually prefaced with the year.

For example: 98/42 **Breakdown of Equipment**   [1998/item 42, this year]

To keep the numbers continuous for the life of the committee. This avoids confusion over numbering at the changeover of years, but means that your numbers can be very long.

For example: 98/8435 **Breakdown of Equipment**   [1998/item 8435]

4.6 Headings and Numbering

Read through the minute item below and:

- insert headings and numbers where appropriate

- show decisions and actions in an appropriate style.

---

8.   **Refurbishment of Meeting Rooms**

The Finance and Management Committees have indicated that approval is likely for a refurbishment programme. The committee have been asked to draw up a proposal, including costings.

It was agreed that the rooms should be co-ordinated in terms of colour and basic equipment and that the two largest rooms should be equipped for training courses, including computer training.

There has been no indication of the figure likely to be approved so it was decided to concentrate on what was needed and divide items into 'essential' and 'desirable'. These will be costed and shown separately in the proposal.

The committee discussed several alternatives and decided that either green or grey-violet were the two most appropriate colours. After considering the overall decor of the building it was decided that a soft green should be used and colour swatches to be obtained by the next meeting (29/10).   *Monica Clarke*

The carpets and curtains have been in place for eight years and are stained and worn. It was decided that their replacement was essential. The committee

---

discussed the style and quality and agreed
that the carpet should be 'tweed' and
should be of a softer quality than the
offices' to create a feeling of quality.
It was agreed to ask potential suppliers
for advice on quality and to obtain
samples for colour by 29 October.   *Huw Davies*

Curtains do not seem appropriate and
should be replaced with blinds.
Catalogues to be collected for next
meeting (29/10) so that options can be
considered.   *Monica Clarke*

The tables are cream in colour and thus
will co-ordinate. They are around six
years old and are getting marked. It
would be preferable to have new ones and
this should be costed. The chairs are a
medley of some original stacking chairs
and left-overs from other offices and some
are breaking. These should be replaced.
Alternatives to be considered from the
furniture catalogues from local suppliers
by the next meeting (29/10).   *Marcus Dowley*

The combination of spot and fluorescent
strip-lighting was agreed to be adequate
but the switches should be altered so that
each lighting system can be turned on
individually and the spotlights should be
on a dimmer system. A quotation to be
sought for 29 October.   *Fran Laurence*

The power and telephone points are well
sited. At present there is only one
computer socket in each meeting room. The
computer department should be asked about
their requirements by 29/10 in order for
Room A to be practical for training
sessions.   *Monica Clarke*

As no member of the committee had specific
knowledge of training, it was decided to
ask some of the regular visiting trainers
for their suggestions on what was
necessary, type, quality, and so on.
Meanwhile, the committee discussed the
standard equipment.

The two existing projectors are old and
unreliable. The two training rooms (A and
F) should each have a projector and a
third can be shared between the other five
rooms. The old machines can be kept as
spares for a year to establish whether
there is a need for additional machines.
The projectors should have suitable stands.

Although paper adds to the cost, it was
decided that flipcharts are more desirable
than whiteboards because of their
flexibility in terms of placement,
portability and the fact that whiteboards
get dirty easily. Each room should have
one flipchart.

The existing video system does not need to
be replaced.

The existing 35mm projector is seldom used
and is in good condition.

5

Writing Clearly and Concisely

5.1 How to Do it

Aim for precision

Avoid vague terms such as 'as soon as possible' or 'when you have time' unless you genuinely do not care when the action is taken (in which case is it worth asking at all?). Give a specific date or time instead.

For example:

> The Security Officer stated that there had been ~~a few~~ *seven* incidents of damage to buildings near the perimeter fence.

> The next meeting should be held ~~as soon as possible~~ *on or before* 28 May.

Similarly, do not use general words such as 'several', 'many', 'long', 'short' or 'a few' as they will mean different things to different people. Instead use specific numbers or quantities.

For example:

> The revised structure will be announced ~~within a few weeks~~ *on (date)*.

If you are referring to documents or papers, always give enough information so that your meaning is clear.

For example:

> Our ~~next~~ 1998 report.

Give full information

If you are giving some information on a subject, make sure you give enough to make its relevance clear.

For example:

> Managers must return the forms by ~~Monday week~~ Monday 4 August.

> Six percent of staff *in the Graphics Department* do not have a contract *of employment*.

Use short words, sentences and paragraphs

Do not use a long word where a short word will do. Similarly, do not use an obscure word where there is a common one available.

For example:

> Mr Prenderghast reported ~~an propitious~~ *a good* start for the suggestion scheme but said that it was necessary to maintain ~~an equipoise~~ *balance* between management authority and the implementation of staff ~~concepts~~ *ideas*.

Ideally sentences should not be more than 20 words long, and to keep to 15 is better. There is nothing wrong with very short sentences provided that there are not too many of them together which makes the text jerky, difficult to read and understand. Sentences that are too long are likely to muddle the reader or to be misread.

Keep paragraphs to a maximum of a quarter of a page. Any longer and they look off-putting. Keep to one subject per paragraph and if you do need to split a long paragraph, find a logical place to do so, rather than splitting it about halfway through.

Always try to have the subject of the paragraph in the first half line or so.

For example:

~~The team spent a considerable~~ ~~amount of time discussing the~~ ~~appointment of an assistant and~~ ...	The appointment of an assistant caused a long discussion and ...

Do not pad out sentences with extra words

Make sure that you are not putting words in that are completely unnecessary. They only cloud the meaning.

For example:

> The group ~~held the suspicion~~ *suspected* that if members referred ~~back~~ to the figures for the last year, they would find the situation had not changed.

> ~~In order~~ to achieve the necessary reduction in paper wastage, the committee felt ~~it was necessary~~ that all members of staff should be reminded about the ~~existence of the~~ recycling scheme.

Use the active voice

The active voice is shorter, more direct and more easily understood than the passive voice.

For example:

~~It was decided by the committee~~	The committee decided
~~that the place of Mark Foxton~~ ...	that Mark Foxton's place ...

Abbreviations, jargon or technical terms

Abbreviations should be given with the full wording in brackets on the first occasion. A glossary explaining technical terms can be added at the end of the minutes if some readers will not understand them. Alternatively, use a footnote to explain them. Try to avoid jargon wherever possible.

Jargon is any term or initials which are understood by a particular group of people and by definition, not by those outside the group.

For example:

•	slang or current buzz words	*spin doctor*
•	use of initials	*PSK, EMD*
•	any 'in' word within a team, department or organisation.	

If you have to use jargon, make sure that it is explained in brackets if it is to be read by anyone outside the group.

Keep to the same tense within a sentence

The tense of a verb tells the time at which the action takes place. The tense must not be changed within a sentence and should not be changed within a paragraph.

For example:

The committee discussed the possibility of developing the scheme and ~~believe~~ *believed* that this should be done by the end of the quarter.

Remember that 'would' is the past tense of 'will'.

For example:

The committee received the report of the finance manager and ~~agree~~ *agreed* that they ~~will~~ *would* reinforce the need for savings at staff briefings.

Remember: minutes are always in the past tense.

5.2 Writing Clearly and Concisely

Work through the exercise below, improving each of the statements.

Not all of the statements are dramatically wrong; most could simply be improved to ensure that the minutes are accurate and easily understood.

If you wish, refer to the notes in the previous section to clarify the problem and possible solution. Model answers are given at the back of the book but you are unlikely to have used exactly the same words. As long as your answer is the same in principle, there is no problem.

1. The Office Manager reported instances of absence as a result of back problems.

    _____

    _____

    _____

2. The committee agreed that the information must be circulated as soon as possible.

    _____

    _____

    _____

3. The new brochure will be published shortly and after the next meeting, the team need not meet for a few months.

    _____

    _____

    _____

4. All members should respond by Friday.

    _____

    _____

    _____

5.   73% of managers cannot load the paper cartridge.

      _____

      _____

6.   It was discussed whether the department could meet the deadline with
      fewer staff.

      _____

      _____

7.   The committee agreed that no one would comprehend the instructions and
      if a response was required from all staff, the wording would need to be
      ameliorated.

      _____

      _____

      _____

      _____

8.   The group were of the opinion that as the team seldom ever achieved their
      target, their systems should be reviewed.

      _____

      _____

      _____

9.   The committee wished to take the opportunity to congratulate Ben Oliver
      and Jerina Khan on their achievement.

      _____

      _____

10.   In order to raise awareness of the scheme, an article should be written for
      the house magazine. To achieve the maximum impact, there should be
      photographs from the exhibition which the committee attended showing the
      committee members talking to a variety of visitors.

      _____

      _____

      _____

      _____

11.   It was decided by the committee that the meeting should be attended by
      Janice Jordan. Her report would be discussed by the committee at the
      November meeting and a plan would be made for future action.

      _____

      _____

      _____

12.   Tom Verity explained that a level playing field was essential for this
      appointment.

      _____

      _____

13.   The committee decided that every entry in the VD system should be
      authorised by a team leader.

      _____

      _____

      _____

14.   The committee agreed that they are willing to consider all suggestions.

      _____

      _____

      _____

      _____

15.   The team agreed that each member will ask six of their staff for
      suggestions.

      _____

      _____

      _____

16.   The Chairman explained that as he is at the Professional Development
      Conference in November, Isobel Laing was chairing the next meeting.

      _____

      _____

      _____

6

Overview and Action Planning

6.1 Overview of Minute Taking

The diagram below recaps the various stages of minute taking and shows at a glance what is involved. The numbers refer to the sections of the **workbook**.

Set agenda

Dispatch agenda

together with any relevant papers or instructions **1.1**

Prepare for Meeting

- book/confirm admin arrangements
- read previous minutes
- check who's who
- read through agenda
- note items to discuss with chairperson
- take supplies
- take minutes for signature
- take additional master copies **2.1**

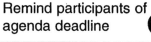

Deadline for agenda **1.1**

Remind participants of agenda deadline **1.1**

Dispatch minutes **4.3**

Dispatch action points

(action minutes) if minutes are delayed **4.3**

After the meeting

- tidy up notes
- write up notes
- pass to chairperson for checking **4** **5**

The meeting

- greet participants
- serve/organise refreshments and supplies
- listen
- summarise **2.2** **3**

6.2 Drawing up an Action Plan

Before you next set up or attend a meeting, reflect on the points you have covered in the workbook. Then, in the spaces below, identify the improvements or actions you would like to take and highlight those that are a priority. Set a date to review those priorities.

The agenda

_____

_____

_____

_____

_____

_____

_____

_____

The meeting

_____

_____

_____

_____

_____

_____

_____

_____

_____

Taking notes

_____

_____

_____

_____

_____

_____

_____

_____

The minutes

_____

_____

_____

_____

_____

Writing clearly and concisely

_____

_____

_____

_____

_____

Return to your action plan after the meeting and make amendments where necessary. Again, set a date to review progress.

6.3 Refining your Technique

When your next set of minutes is typed and approved, return to your notes and highlight (ideally with a fluorescent marker) those notes which you actually used in the final minutes.

If you continue to do this every time you take minutes you will find that you become aware of the notes you will be highlighting as you write them. From there it is just one stage to writing only what you know you will highlight.

It is probably unrealistic to hope for a full page of highlighted notes. However, you should find that the proportion of highlighted words increases with every set of minutes.

Although this is a chore to do, it is a very effective method of improving your note taking.

7
Model Answers

Section 1.3
Preparing an Agenda
(page 9)

Full agenda

FUNDAY PLANNING GROUP

21st June 19XX, 3.45pm

Meeting Room J10

AGENDA

1. **Apologies for absence**

2. **Minutes of previous meeting**

3. **Matters arising**

4. **Venue**

5. **Entertainment for children**

6. **Refreshments**

   6.1 Lunch arrangements

   6.2 Caterers

   6.3 Bar opening times

   6.4 Bar subsidy

7. **Timetable**

8. **Publicity**

   8.1 Planning the event (house magazine)

   8.2 Write-up for French magazine

9. **Guests from other divisions**

10. **Any other business**

11. **Next meeting**

Objectives agenda

FUNDAY PLANNING GROUP

21st June 19XX, 3.45pm

Meeting Room J10

AGENDA

1. Apologies for absence

2. Minutes of previous meeting

3. Venue

    to agree alternative venue

4. Entertainment for children

    to decide on entertainment for the children

5. Refreshments

    to decide format of lunch

    to agree who will provide catering

    to agree bar opening times

    to fix level of bar subsidy

6. Timetable

    to set timetable for the day

7. Publicity

    to nominate author of article for house magazine

    to nominate author of article for French division's magazine

8. Guests from other divisions

    to agree policy on inviting guests from European divisions

9. Any other business

10. Next meeting

Note: The points within the sections are generally unnumbered in this style of agenda, but may be numbered according to personal preference (see page 6).

Section 3.2
Subject and
Viewpoint (page 27)

1.   "I think we should introduce a 'post-in' system so that we can easily track all mail."

> *Subject:*   *Post-in system*
>
> *Viewpoint:*   *In favour*

2.   "Tom came to see me yesterday and asked what we are going to do about the Christmas shut down."

> *Subject:*   *Christmas shut down*
>
> *Viewpoint:*   *Not given*

3.   "None of my staff like the idea of an open-plan office and I am having a hard time convincing them of the benefits. I think we should reconsider."

> *Subject:*   *Open-plan office*
>
> *Viewpoint:*   *Should reconsider*

4.   "Jackie is a fine manager and her tactful approach has worked wonders on morale in that department."

> *Subject:*   *Jackie*
>
> *Viewpoint:*   *Is good manager*

5.   "If we allow the flexitime to be extended to administrative staff, there will be no stopping it. Soon the production lines will be stopping and starting at random."

> *Subject:*   *Extension of flexitime*
>
> *Viewpoint:*   *Against*

Section 3.3
Summarising a Report
(page 28)

Annual Report: Health and Safety

There were four accidents that resulted in absence from work; there was no Company liability for any of these.

The training programme finished in March with 30% of employees still to attend. The programme is to be repeated for these staff, together with half-day refresher sessions for those who did attend and courses on specific subjects as required.

Section 3.5
Taking Notes
(page 34)

Simple scribble

WATER MACHINES	
A	saw machine at a supplier
N	good idea
A	put them in meeting rooms
L	cost?
N	less than now
L	cost?
A	rent – £3 £7 per bottle
N	use more water?
L	not drunk for sake of it
S	will have to raise room hire
L	OK for this year bigger raise next year
Andy	who responsible for replacing bottles – heavy
A	caretakers?
L	will do and catering will buy
Chair	install machines in all seven rooms negotiate price caterers responsible for maintenance
Action:	Liz report back installed ASAP forewarn caterers

For and against

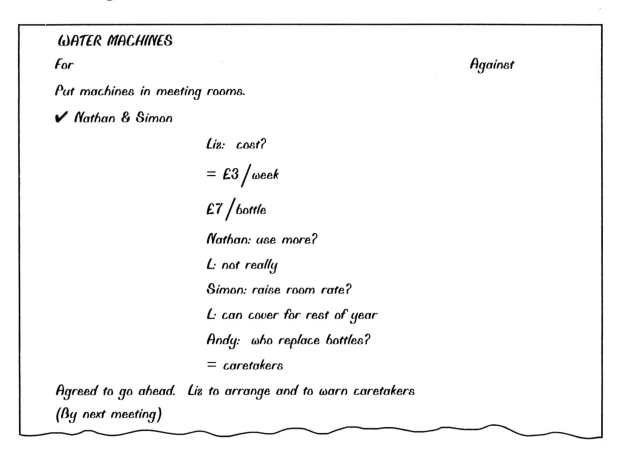

Subject structure

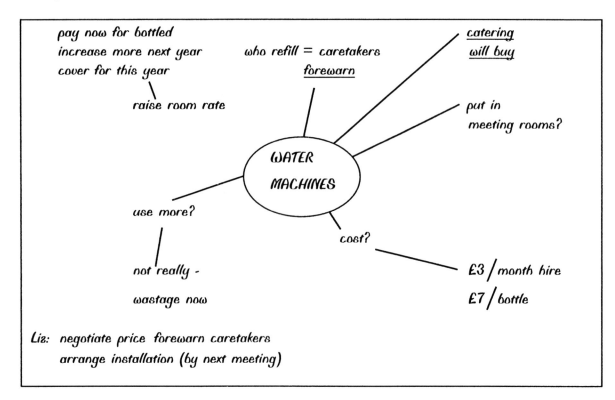

Section 4.2
Using the Styles
(page 43)

1a Verbatim

John Carter suggested that staff on grades one to four be allowed to take unofficial flexitime of up to one hour on a Friday afternoon. There were concerns about cover and it was suggested that this might extend to full-scale flexitime. However, the idea was supported by Malcolm Bowden who pointed out that it was not a major perk and some departments operated the system already.

Because of concerns about staff disappearing at any time, the proposal was agreed providing that it is limited to one hour on a Friday and that the secretaries arrange cover between themselves.

1b Summary

The committee discussed offering staff on grades one to four time off in lieu. Although there were concerns that this might lead to full-scale flexitime, it was agreed to allow these staff to take up to one hour in lieu on a Friday afternoon, provided that cover was arranged.

1c Action

The committee agreed to allow staff on grades one to four to take up to one hour in lieu on a Friday afternoon, provided that cover was arranged.

2a Verbatim

The installation of chilled drinking water machines in the meeting rooms was suggested. The rental of the unit is £3 with a charge per bottle of £7 and the cost is likely to be similar to that of bottled water but there should be less wastage.

The possibility of using more water was discussed but was felt not to be important as there is considerable wastage with bottled water. The impact on room-hire rates was raised and it was agreed that this should be borne from the catering budget for the remainder of the current year. The next increase will be greater to cover the cost but this is not expected to cause complaint as users do not complain about the charge for bottled water.

Maintenance can be carried out by the caretakers, who will need to be forewarned and catering will arrange for the buying of water bottles.

> *Action:*   *Liz, by next meeting.*

2b Summary

The committee discussed the possibility of installing chilled drinking water machines in the seven meeting rooms. The cost is unlikely to be greater than the bottled water and can be covered from the catering budget for the remainder of the year. The room rate will be increased to cover the cost at the normal time. The machines could be maintained by the caretakers and ordering would be handled by catering.

> *Agreed:* *To install machines in all seven meeting rooms as soon as possible.*
>
> *To forewarn caretakers regarding maintenance.*
>
> *Action:* *Liz, by next meeting.*

(Note: The decision is shown in two different ways in the above examples, simply to indicate the alternatives.)

2c Action

The committee decided to install chilled drinking water machines in all seven meeting rooms, to be maintained by caretakers with buying arranged by catering.

> *Action:* *Liz, by next meeting.*

Section 4.6
Headings and
Numbering (page 55)

8.   Refurbishment of Meeting Rooms

The Finance and Management Committees have indicated that approval is likely for a refurbishment programme. The committee have been asked to draw up a proposal, including costings.

It was agreed that the rooms should be co-ordinated in terms of colour and basic equipment and that the two largest rooms should be equipped for training courses, including computer training.

8.1   Budget

There has been no indication of the figure likely to be approved so it was decided to concentrate on what was needed and divide items into 'essential' and 'desirable'. These will be costed and shown separately in the proposal.

8.2   Colour scheme

The committee discussed several alternatives and decided that either green or grey-violet were the two most appropriate colours. After considering the overall decor of the building it was decided that a soft green should be used. Colour swatches to be obtained.

Decided: *To obtain colour swatches for paint.*

Action: *Monica Clarke   29 October*

8.3   Fixtures and fittings

(a)   CARPETS AND CURTAINS

The carpets and curtains have been in place for eight years and are stained and worn. It was decided that their replacement was essential. The committee discussed the style and quality and agreed that the carpets should be 'tweed' and should be of a softer quality than the offices, to create a feeling of quality.

Decided: *To obtain samples for carpets and ask suppliers for advice on quality.*

Action: *Huw Davies   29 October*

Curtains do not seem appropriate and should be replaced with blinds.

Decided: *To obtain catalogues for blinds.*

Action: *Monica Clarke   29 October*

b)   TABLES AND CHAIRS

The tables are cream in colour and thus will co-ordinate. They are around six years old and are getting marked. It would be preferable to have new ones and this should be costed. The chairs are a medley of some original stacking chairs and left-overs from other offices and some are breaking. These should be replaced.

Decided: *To obtain catalogues for both tables and chairs.*

Action: *Marcus Dowley   29 October*

(c)   LIGHTING

The combination of spot and fluorescent strip-lighting was agreed to be adequate but the switches should be altered so that each lighting system can be turned on individually and the spotlights should be on a dimmer system.

Decided: *To obtain quotation for changing switching.*

Action: *Fran Laurence   29 October*

(d)   POWER, TELEPHONE AND COMPUTER POINTS

The power and telephone points are well sited. At present there is only one computer socket in each meeting room. The computer department should be asked about their requirements in order for Room A to be practical for training sessions.

Decided: *To consult computer department.*

Action: *Monica Clarke   29 October*

8.4 Training equipment

As no member of the committee had specific knowledge of training it was decided to ask some of the regular visiting trainers for their suggestions on what was necessary – type, quality, and so on. Meanwhile, the committee discussed the standard equipment.

(a)   OVERHEAD PROJECTOR

The two existing projectors are old and unreliable. The two training rooms (A and F) should each have a projector and a third can be shared between the other five rooms. The old machines can be kept as spares for a year to establish whether there is a need for additional machines. The projectors should have suitable stands.

(b)   FLIPCHART/WHITEBOARD

Although flipchart paper adds to the cost, it was decided that flipcharts are more desirable than whiteboards because of their flexibility in terms of placement, portability and the fact that whiteboards get dirty easily. Each room should have one flipchart.

(c)   VIDEO

The existing video system does not need to be replaced.

(d)   35mm SLIDE PROJECTOR

The existing 35mm projector is seldom used and in good condition.

Section 5.2
Writing Clearly and
Concisely (page 64)

1. The Office Manager reported nine instances of absence as a result of back problems.

2. The committee agreed that the information must be circulated before the end of February.

3. The new brochure will be published on 4 September. After the next meeting the team need not meet until June 1999.

4. All members should respond by Friday 19 May.

5. 73% of middle managers in this division cannot load the paper cartridge.

6. The committee discussed whether the department could meet the deadline with fewer staff.

    or

    The probability of the department meeting the deadline with fewer staff was considered.

7. The committee agreed that no one would understand the instructions and if an answer was needed from all staff, the wording would need to be improved.

8. The group believed that as the team seldom achieved their target, their systems should be reviewed.

9. The committee congratulated Ben Oliver and Jerina Khan on their achievement.

10. To raise awareness of the scheme, an article should be written for the house magazine. To achieve the maximum impact, there should be photographs from the exhibition showing the committee members talking to visitors.

11. The committee decided that Janice Jordan should attend the meeting. They would discuss her report at the November meeting and plan future action.

12. Tom Verity explained that every applicant should have an equal chance.

13. The committee decided that every entry in the Vehicle Driver system should be authorised by a team leader.

14. The committee agreed that they were willing to consider all suggestions.

15.   The team agreed that each member would ask six of their staff for suggestions.

16.   The Chairman explained that, as he would be at the Professional Development Conference in November, Isobel Laing would chair the next meeting.

8
Index